The Guitar
TRAVIS **PICKING**
SONGBOOK

Learn 12 popular songs arranged for solo Travis picking guitar

DARYL**KELLIE**

FUNDAMENTAL**CHANGES**

The Guitar Travis Picking Songbook

Learn 12 popular songs arranged for solo Travis picking guitar

ISBN: 978-1-78933-370-1

Published by **www.fundamental-changes.com**

www.fundamental-changes.com

Over 11,000 fans on Facebook: **FundamentalChangesInGuitar**

Instagram: **FundamentalChanges**

For over 350 Free Guitar Lessons with Videos Check Out

www.fundamental-changes.com

Cover Image Copyright: Shutterstock – Virrage Images

Contents

Contents

Introduction

I first became aware of Travis picking when I heard the late great Chet Atkins. My first thought was that I was listening to *two* guitars playing. Surely, he must have overdubbed these complex syncopated melodies, chords and basslines?! When I discovered he was playing all the parts simultaneously on one guitar my mind was blown!

And so began my obsession with Travis picking. I bought a thumb pick and began working my way through the repertoire of players like Merle Travis (the man responsible for the name of this technique), right through to modern virtuoso players like Tommy Emmanuel.

In this book I'll teach you how to play twelve classic tunes, all arranged for Travis picking, and break down how to play each technique step-by-step. I recommend you use a thumb pick in order to achieve the classic *boom chick* sound (more on that later) and a more authentic feel.

Top Tip! If you are new to Travis picking and your thumb pick catches on the strings or feels particularly cumbersome, feel free to file it down a little.

I've recorded every track for you and the audio can be downloaded from **www.fundamental-changes.com**. You'll hear every example in the book, but it also makes a lovely album of tunes, even if I say so myself!

Lastly, this book often refers to the picking fingers and to do this I use the conventional *p i m a* names.

Thumb = *p*

Index = *i*

Middle = *m*

Ring finger = *a*

Happy pickin'!

Daryl Kellie

October 2021

Get the Audio

The audio files for this book are available to download for free from **www.fundamental-changes.com.** The link is in the top right-hand corner. Simply select this book title from the drop-down menu and follow the instructions to get the audio.

We recommend that you download the files directly to your computer, not to your tablet, and extract them there before adding them to your media library. You can then put them on your tablet, iPod or burn them to CD. On the download page there is a help PDF and we also provide technical support via the contact form.

For over 350 free lessons with videos check out:

www.fundamental-changes.com

Join our active Facebook community:

www.facebook.com/groups/fundamentalguitar

Tag us for a share on Instagram: **FundamentalChanges**

Chapter 1 – American Folk Medley

This first arrangement is a great place to start if you're new to Travis picking, as it begins with a simple, and typical, Travis picking pattern.

Look at the notation below. All the notes with tails pointing down should be picked with the thumb (*p*), and those with the tails pointing up should be picked with the fingers (*i, m* and *a*).

Primer Exercises

Palm-mute the bass strings slightly to create the iconic, punchy *boom chick* sound. The *boom* refers to sound of the bass strings being struck with the thumb, the *chick* refers to the higher strings or string (string 4 in this instance) also picked with the thumb.

Example 1a

In bar 17 the melody dips down onto the lower strings which are usually reserved for the bass. In this instance, alternate pick the melody notes but be sure to keep the Travis groove going unhindered.

Example 1b

The feel changes in bar 32 and you will need to play a with a more syncopated (off beat) swung feel in the picking fingers. This melodic syncopation over the rigid boom chick makes the swing feel much more apparent and is widely used by many of the top Travis pickers.

Example 1c

Here's the full arrangement…

Example 1d

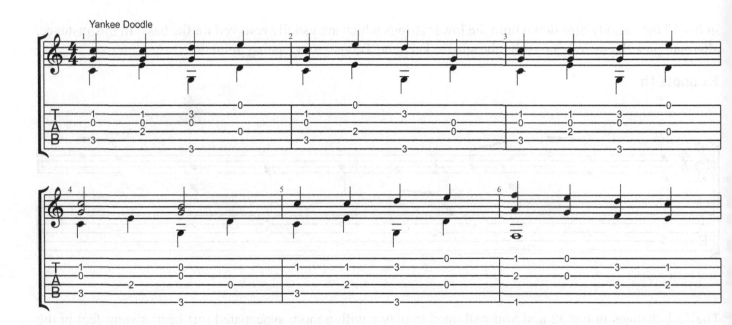

Oh Susanna

Turkey in the Straw

When the Saints Go Marching In

10

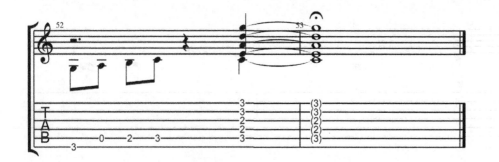

Chapter 2 – New World Theme

Dvorak's *New World Symphony* is a well-known orchestral piece and this cheeky little arrangement of the main theme is quite a departure from the original. When played with Travis picking technique, it has a great bounce and is really fun to play. This version uses a capo on the third fret and many familiar open chord shapes.

Primer Exercises

In bar nineteen, keep the second and third fingers held down from the preceding C chord shape and use the first and fourth fingers to fret melody notes on the high strings.

Example 2a

In bar thirty-one, anchor the second finger on the second string, while the first and third fingers hammer-on and pull-off on the third string.

Example 2b

The arrangement concludes with a lush run of *natural harmonics*. Gently touch the first and fourth fingers onto the string (without pushing the string down) directly above the 7th and 12th frets above the capo. (Be mindful that the capo has "moved" the natural harmonics up three frets to the 10th and 15th frets).

Example 2c

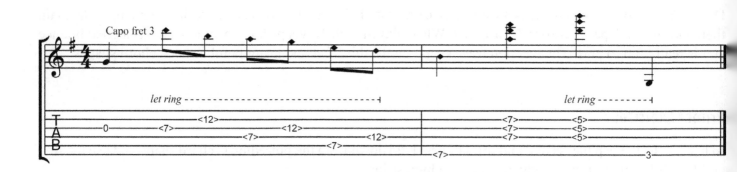

Here's the full arrangement…

Example 2d

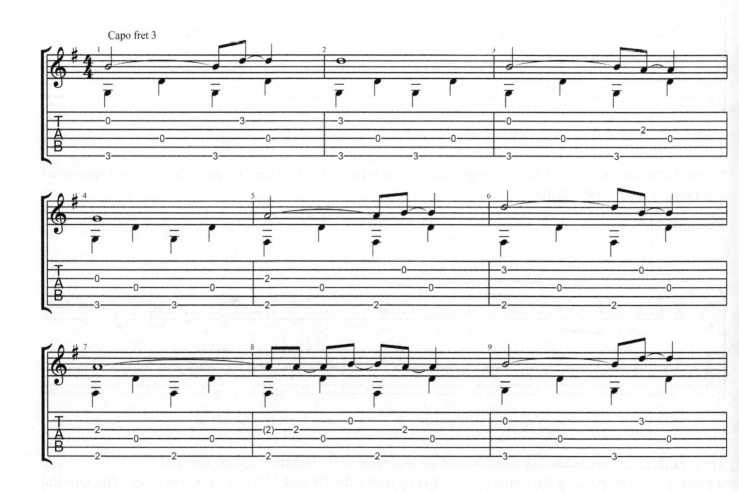

15

Chapter 3 – Waltzing Matilda

The "bush ballad" *Waltzing Matilda* is considered to be the unofficial national anthem of Australia, and is featured here as a tribute to one of the great Travis Pickers of our time, Australian virtuoso Tommy Emmanuel.

This is the first of the arrangements in this book to use Drop-D tuning (tune your low E down to D). You will also need to place a capo at the 3rd fret.

Primer Exercises

The intro features a tricky syncopated line played by the fingers while the thumb holds down a steady boom chick. Look carefully at the notation and notice where the high part fits *between* the low part.

If you count the 1/16th notes like this:

1 e & a 2 e & a 3 e & a 4 e & a.

Then the rhythm you pick with your fingers falls on these divisions of the beat:

1 e **& a** 2 **e &** a **3 e** & **a** 4 e & a.

Example 3a

The melody begins in bar five. Use an open D chord shape with the first, second and third fingers, just as you would in standard tuning. However, when you reach bar seven, use the first finger to barre the 2nd fret. This allows you to reach the 5th fret with your fourth finger.

Example 3b

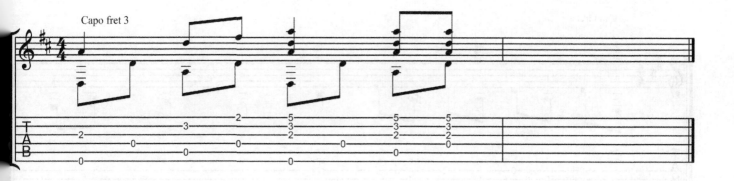

The interlude from bar twenty-one features lots of *ornaments* (the smaller notes in the notation and tab). In bar twenty-one these are hammer-ons and pull-offs, but in bar twenty-two and twenty-three they are slides. Use your first finger to slide between the notes here.

Example 3c

The natural harmonics in bar twenty-five have open strings in the bass, but those in bar twenty-six are played with *fretted notes* underneath. To do this, fret the bass note with your third finger while your first finger lays *gently* over the 7th fret (10th fret with the capo). Pick the bass notes with the thumb and natural harmonics with the fingers.

Combining harmonics and fretted notes simultaneously may take a few tries but persevere and you will soon find the correct amount of pressure needed.

Example 3d

Here's the full arrangement…

Example 3e

Da Coda

D.S. al Coda

Chapter 4 – Korobeiniki

Here is an arrangement of a traditional Russian melody that you might just recognise!

Primer Exercises

The chord shapes are all very familiar, beginning with an open E major. As the melody climbs to the note C, barre your first finger slightly to allow the 1st fret on both the third and second strings to sound.

Example 4a

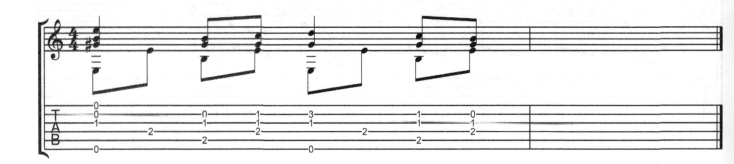

Hold down the chord shapes (E and Am) for the whole bar, using the fourth finger to reach the additional melody notes.

Example 4b

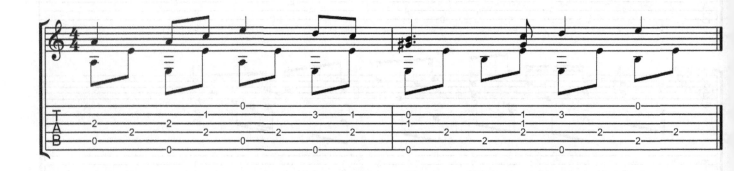

The fast 1/16th note licks in bar sixteen are played with pull-offs (use the first and fourth fingers to allow for the big stretch) while the ones in bar seventeen will require you to hold down a diminished chord shape – first on the 6th and 7th fret, then slide the whole shape up to the 9th and 10th fret.

Example 4c

Now here's the full arrangement...

Example 4d

26

Chapter 5 – Limehouse Blues

Contrary to what the name suggests, *Limehouse Blues* is not a typical 12-bar-blues, but the dominant 7th chords and *twos-feel* groove make it a great fun tune to Travis Pick.

Primer Exercises

In the opening melody, the accompaniment is based on an open C chord shape. Notice how the third finger must swap between the fifth and sixth strings to play the bassline while the third finger remains static.

The notes on the first string are played with the first and fourth finger. This may seem like a squeeze at first and might require a few tries to play it cleanly, particularly when you realise that you need to avoid the second string completely.

Example 5a

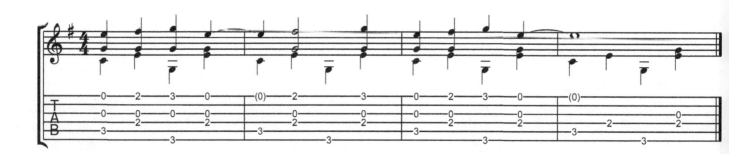

The harmonics in bar eleven are all *natural harmonics*, but to be able to play the 7th and 12th fret harmonics simultaneously you need to use your first and fourth finger.

Example 5b

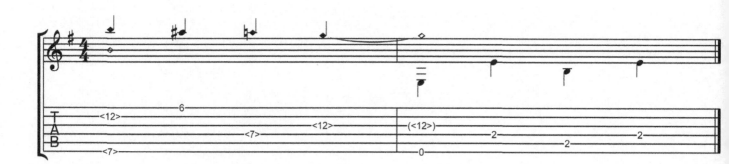

Bar thirty-three contains an unusual chromatic part on the high strings while the bassline continues uninterrupted. To do this, hook your thumb over the neck and use it to play the bass note on the 8th fret.

You may have seen Tommy Emmanuel and Chet Atkins use this trick. It's a great technique that allows you play moving chord or lead parts over the top of a constant bass-note.

Example 5c

Now here's the full arrangement…

Example 5d

Chapter 6 – Air on the G String

Bach's *Air on the G String* is perhaps one of the most iconic orchestral pieces of all time. This arrangement is in Drop-D tuning and has a folk-like bounce when Travis picked.

Primer Exercises

The opening two bars should be played with a partial barre on the 2nd fret. This allows you to make very small adjustments to play the changing notes while maintaining the sustained D major shape on the high strings.

Example 6a

In bar seventeen the thumb picking pattern stops for a lick that you must let ring. Notice how the notes (including harmonics) are on different strings to allow for this. Pick them all clearly and be sure to avoid any accidental muting.

Example 6b

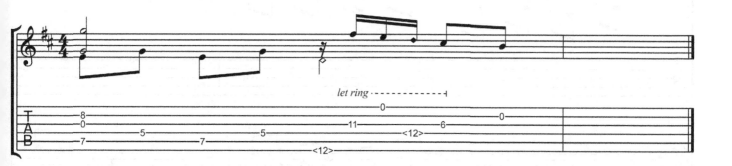

Bar twenty-one uses a similar idea, this time extended to play part of a B minor scale lick. You'll need to stretch the left hand a little to sustain these notes.

To play the B minor "harmonics chord" at the end, use your third finger on the 9th fret while your first finger barres the 7th fret (*lightly* touching the strings in line with the fret wire to allow the harmonics to sound).

Example 6c

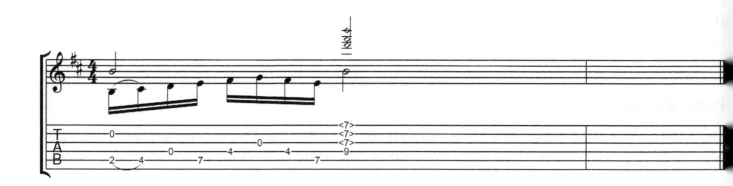

Now here's the full arrangement…

Example 6d

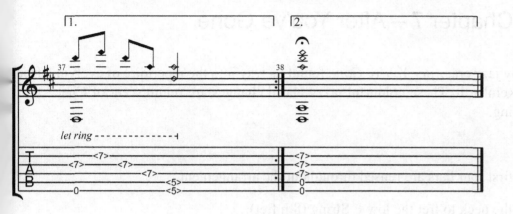

Chapter 7 – After You've Gone

An absolute classic of the early jazz era, *After You've Gone* found its way into the repertoire of everyone from Louis Armstrong to Django Reinhardt. These colourful jazzy chord changes are reminiscent of Chet Atkins when played with Travis picking.

Primer Exercises

The chord shapes used in the first four bars are reused throughout the arrangement.

- The thumb comes over the neck to fret the low E String (8th fret)

- The second and third fingers remain on the two middle strings

- The first and fourth fingers play all of the melody notes on strings one and two.

Notice how the second finger must move down to the 8th fret for the third and fourth bar. This will be quite a stretch, especially with the thumb note on the sixth string.

Example 7a

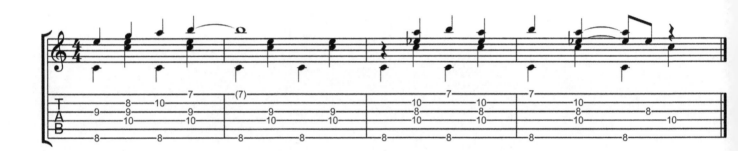

Remember that the picking hand fingers are named,

Thumb = *p*

Index = *i*

Middle = *m*

Ring finger = *a*

In bar fifty-seven the picking switches to a *p i m, p i a* pattern.

Notice how these groups of three cut across the 4/4 beat. This can be tricky to get up to speed, so start slowly at around 100 bpm and build you speed and finger independence gradually.

This idea is based on the middle section of *Cannonball Rag* by Merle Travis.

Example 7b

Now here's the full arrangement…

Example 7c

Da Coda

D.C. al Coda

Chapter 8 – I'll See You In My Dreams

I'll See You In My Dreams is a popular song, written by Isham Jones and Gus Kahn in 1924 and was later recorded by Django Reinhardt, which in turn inspired Merle Travis' rendition. Since then, the likes of Chet Atkins and Thom Bresh have both recorded their own versions and it has become something of a Travis picking standard.

Primer Exercises

Notice how the opening chord pattern uses the same chord shapes and tricks as those at the start of *After You've Gone*. The thumb frets the low E string, the second and third fingers are on the two middle strings, and the first and fourth fingers deal with the melody.

Example 8a

In bars fourteen and fifteen, play a G major barre chord shape at the 3rd fret, but pivot the barre up to allow for the occasional open strings to sound.

Keep the tip of the finger anchored on the sixth string.

Example 8b

Pick the fast triplets in bar twenty-five with a *p i m* pattern. Rather than using a barre, use your thumb over the neck to fret the sixth string for the D7b9 chord. This allows you to lift off a finger as you pick the 19th fret natural harmonic immediately after.

Example 8c

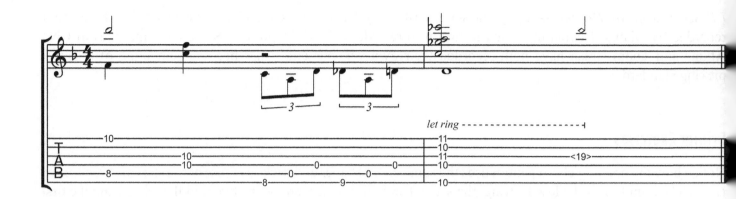

From bar thirty-four, use your fourth finger to play the bends. I use my thumb on the sixth string to give my left hand a better position for the bends. It's a great little trick to spice up your picking patterns. Try it on a few other chord shapes up and down the neck, once you have it under your fingers, to incorporate it into your own patterns.

Example 8d

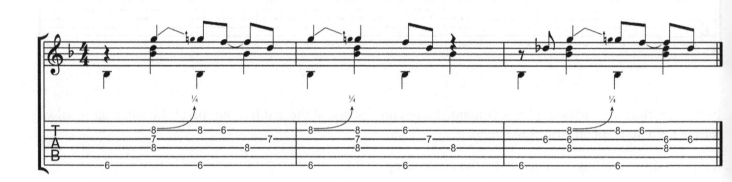

In bar forty-six, use the first finger to fret the fifth string, and rest the third finger gently across the 12th fret for the natural harmonics.

Example 8e

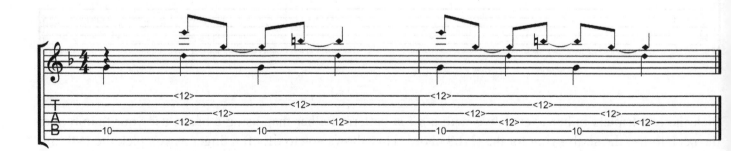

Now here's the full arrangement…

Example 8f

Da Coda

50

D.S. al Coda

Chapter 9 – Dinah

Dinah was first recorded in the 1920s and was included in the show *Kid Boots*. Like many show tunes of that era it was soon absorbed into the jazz repertoire and played by the likes of Louis Armstrong, Duke Ellington and Fats Waller to name but a few.

Primer Exercises

For the opening A6 chord, use the first, second and third fingers. In bar two, remove the first finger from that shape to fret the 5th fret melody note on the first string. Finally, put it back on the third string and add the fourth finger on the 9th fret to form the final shape in bar two.

Example 9a

Bars five and six include some barre chords and big stretches. You may need to practice these separately at first to build the left-hand strength and ensure a clean execution.

Example 9b

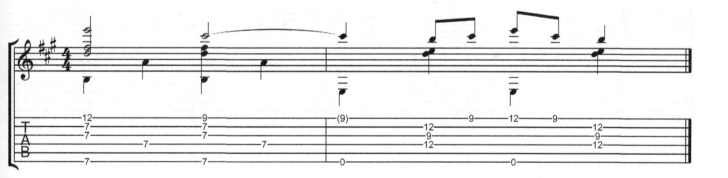

Bar twenty-four features a lick that combines *artificial harmonics* and non-harmonics. Use your index finger over the 19th fret node point as your thumb picks the string, with your ring finger following in a parallel motion two strings away.

Example 9c

Here's the full arrangement...

Example 9d

Chapter 10 – Dance of the Sugar Plum Fairy

This tune is taken from Tchaikovsky's ballet, *The Nutcracker*. Upon its first performance in 1892, it only received modest success. However, it found its way into popular culture after Walt Disney used it in his 1940 animated movie *Fantasia*.

The intro of this arrangement is inspired by Tommy Emmanuel's fast open string licks. (Check out his intro on *Train to Dusseldorf*!)

Primer Exercises

Use slight Palm-muting in bar two and gradually release the mute throughout the lick.

The trick to achieving speed here is to use a *pivot finger*. For example, in bar two, my third finger never leaves the second string. It simply slides between the 5th and 4th fret. All the work is done by the first finger pulling-off.

Example 10a

The fast arpeggio in bar twenty-three is played with a swift *p i m a* action. Palm-mute the strings slightly to get a clean, tight sound.

Example 10b

This fast E Natural Minor run is played with the sustain technique described in Example 6b. Notes are played on adjacent strings to allow them to ring into each other but here the technique is executed much more quickly.

Begin by using the *p i m* pattern shown and decide for yourself how the pattern should continue.

Example 10c

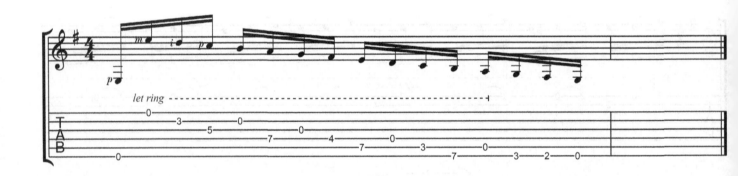

Now here's the full arrangement…

Example 10d

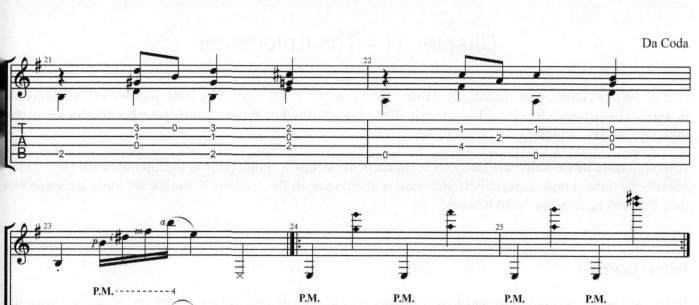

Da Coda

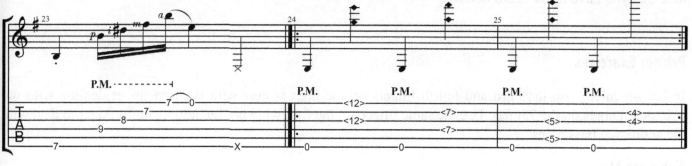

D.S. al Coda

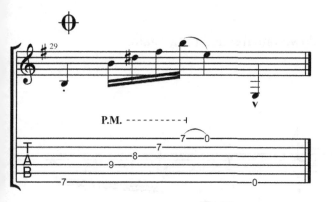

Chapter 11 – The Entertainer

One of the most iconic piano pieces of all time, *The Entertainer* was written by Scott Joplin and first published in 1902. The *two-step* feel is typical of early 20th century Ragtime music, which later became an important influence on Travis picking.

Although none of the individual sections seem particularly challenging, putting together the entire piece may initially be quite a task, especially if you want to memorise all the sections. Chances are there are some bits here that you have never heard before!

Primer Exercises

In bar seventeen use the third and fourth fingers on the high strings with the first finger dealing with the occasional notes on the 7th fret. Use the same fingers in the following bar but add the third finger to deal with the additional bass notes.

Example 11a

In bar forty-four, slide the entire B minor barre chord shape down one fret and back again.

Example 11b

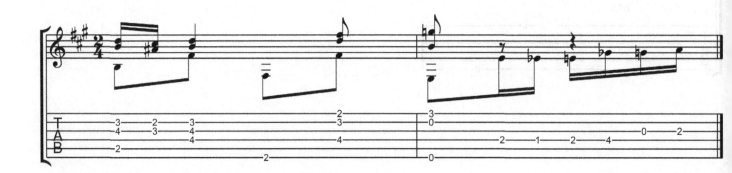

In bar sixty-three, notice how the entire D6 chord shape slides down one fret and back. All you need to do is remove the fourth finger when you want the open A string to sound.

I use this trick many times during the arrangement.

Example 11c

Now here's the full arrangement…

Example 11d

Da Coda

Chapter 12 – Rondo Alla Turca

Mozart's *Turkish Rondo* is one of his best-known piano pieces. The energetic pace and cheeky melodies make it a really fun tune to Travis pick and here I have arranged the most famous sections. It's not the longest arrangement in this book, but it's certainly the toughest to bring up to speed!

Primer Exercises

Play the first part with your first and third fingers held in place on the two middle strings at the 5th and 7th fret. All the other fretted notes are played with the second and fourth finger.

Example 12a

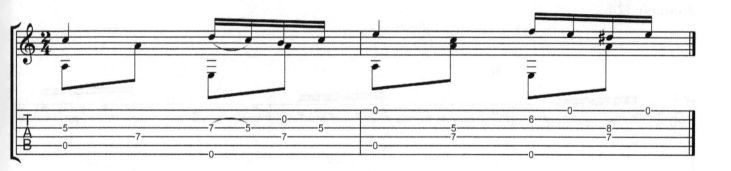

To build speed on the next part of the melody you'll find it helpful to alternate your picking finger on the second string with a simple *i m i m* pattern.

Example 12b

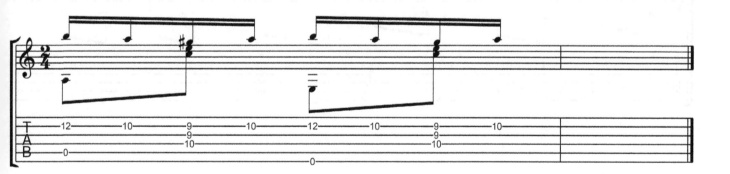

The C and G major chords in the second section are played with the thumb hooked over the neck to fret the sixth strings to allow the open string to sound.

Example 12c

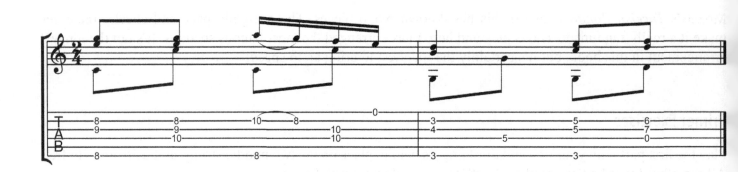

Now here's the full arrangement…

Example 12d

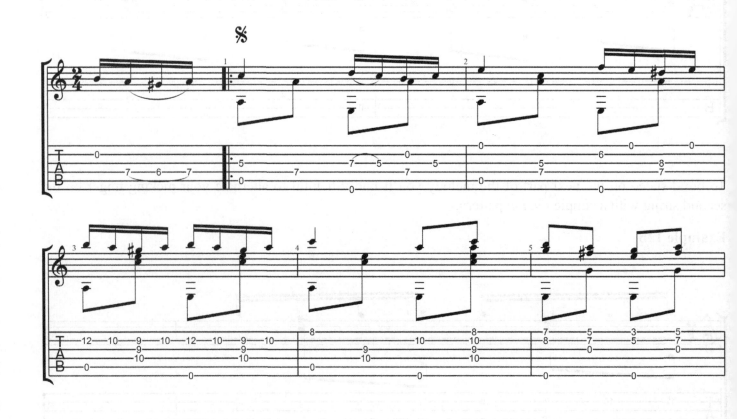

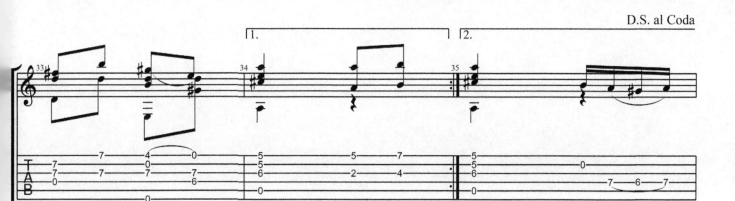

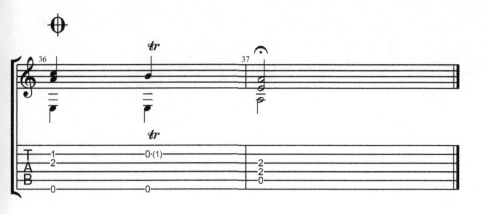

Made in the USA
Middletown, DE
03 November 2024

63791486R00044